W9-ARU-864

BASEBALL LEGENDS

Hank Aaron
Grover Cleveland Alexander
Ernie Banks
Johnny Bench
Yogi Berra
Roy Campanella
Roberto Clemente
Ty Cobb
Dizzy Dean
Joe DiMaggio
Bob Feller
Jimmie Foxx
Lou Gehrig
Bob Gibson
Rogers Hornsby
Walter Johnson
Sandy Koufax
Mickey Mantle
Christy Mathewson
Willie Mays
Stan Musial
Satchel Paige
Brooks Robinson
Frank Robinson
Jackie Robinson
Babe Ruth
Duke Snider
Warren Spahn
Willie Stargell
Honus Wagner
Ted Williams
Carl Yastrzemski
Cy Young

CHELSEA HOUSE PUBLISHERS

CUBS

BASEBALL LEGENDS

GROVER CLEVELAND ALEXANDER

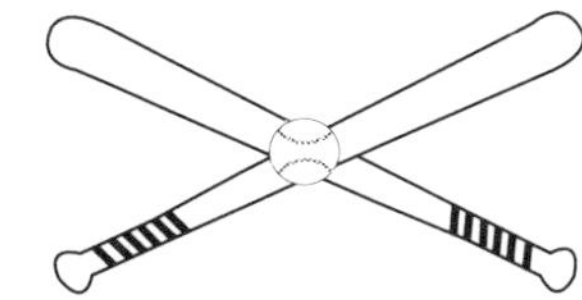

Jack Kavanagh

Introduction by
Jim Murray

Senior Consultant
Earl Weaver

CHELSEA HOUSE PUBLISHERS
New York • Philadelphia

Published by arrangement with
Chelsea House Publishers.
Newfield Publications is a federally
registered trademark of Newfield
Publications, Inc.

Produced by James Charlton Associates
New York, New York.

Designed by Hudson Studio
Ossining, New York.

Typesetting by LinoGraphics
New York, New York.

Picture research by Jennie McGregor
Cover illustration by Dan O'Leary

Library of Congress Cataloging-in-Publication Data

Kavanagh, Jack.
Grover Cleveland Alexander/Jack Kavanagh;
introduction by Jim Murray.
p. cm.—(Baseball legends)
Includes bibliographical references.
Summary: Follows the life of the talented baseball pitcher from its beginning to the sunset years.
ISBN 0-7910-1166-6
ISBN 0-7910-1200-X (pbk.)
1. Alexander, Grover Cleveland, 1887-1950—Juvenile literature. 2. Baseball players—United States—Biography—Juvenile literature. [1. Alexander, Grover Cleveland, 1887-1950. 2. Baseball players.] I. Title.
II. Series.
GV865.A33K38 1990
92—dc20
[796.357'092]
[B]

CONTENTS

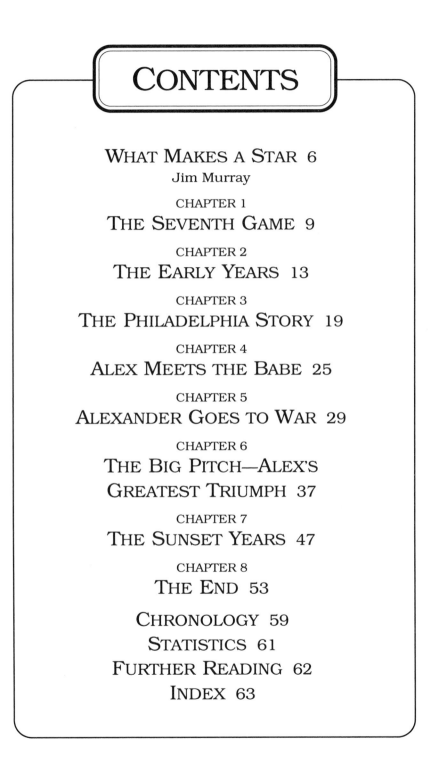

WHAT MAKES A STAR

Jim Murray

No one has ever been able to explain to me the mysterious alchemy that makes one man a .350 hitter and another player, more or less identical in physical makeup, hard put to hit .200. You look at an Al Kaline, who played with the Detroit Tigers from 1953 to 1974. He was pale, stringy, almost poetic-looking. He always seemed to be struggling against a bad case of mononucleosis. But with a bat in his hands, he was King Kong. During his career, he hit 399 home runs, rapped out 3,007 hits, and compiled a .297 batting average.

Form isn't the reason. The first time anybody saw Roberto Clemente step into the batter's box for the Pittsburgh Pirates, the best guess was that Clemente would be back in Double A ball in a week. He had one foot in the bucket and held his bat at an awkward angle—he looked as though he couldn't hit an outside pitch. A lot of other ballplayers may have had a better-looking stance. Yet they never led the National League in hitting in four different years, the way Clemente did.

Not every ballplayer is born with the ability to hit a curveball. Nor is exceptional hand-eye coordination the key to heavy hitting. Big-league locker rooms are filled with players who have all the attributes, save one: discipline. Every baseball man can tell you a story about a pitcher who throws a ball faster than anyone has ever seen but who has no control on or *off* the field.

The Hall of Fame is full of people who transformed themselves into great ballplayers by working at the sport, by studying the game, and making sacrifices. They're overachievers—and winners. If you want to find them, just watch the World Series. Or simply read about New York Yankee great Lou Gehrig; Ted Williams, "the Splendid Splinter" of the Boston Red Sox; or the Dodgers' strikeout king Sandy Koufax.

A pitcher *should* be able to win a lot of ballgames with a 98-miles-per-hour fastball. But what about the pitcher who wins 20 games a year with a fastball so slow that you can catch it with your teeth? Bob Feller of the Cleveland Indians got into the Hall of Fame with a blazing fastball that glowed in the dark. National League star Grover Cleveland Alexander got there with a pitch that took considerably longer to reach the plate; but when it did arrive, the pitch was exactly where Alexander wanted it to be—and the last place the batter expected it to be.

There are probably more players with exceptional ability who didn't make it to the major leagues than there are who did. A number of great hitters, bored with fielding practice, had to be dropped from their team because their home-run production didn't make up for their lapses in the field. And then there are players like Brooks Robinson of the Baltimore Orioles, who made himself into a human vacuum cleaner at third base because he knew that working hard to become an expert fielder would win him a job in the big leagues.

A star is not something that flashes through the sky. That's a comet. Or a meteor. A star is something you can steer ships by. It stays in place and gives off a steady glow; it is fixed, permanent. A star works at being a star.

And that's how you tell a star in baseball. He shows up night after night and takes pride in how brightly he shines. He's Willie Mays running so hard his hat keeps falling off; Ty Cobb sliding to stretch a single into a double; Lou Gehrig, after being fooled in his first two at-bats, belting the next pitch off the light tower because he's taken the time to study the pitcher. Stars never take themselves for granted. That's why they're stars.

1 THE SEVENTH GAME

It's a long way from the bullpens at Yankee Stadium to the pitcher's mound. In 1926 the distance was even greater than it is today—and a player didn't ride in a cart. He walked.

As a reliever in the seventh game of the World Series, Grover Cleveland Alexander walked to the mound very slowly. His aged arm should have been tired out, since the day before he had pitched the St. Louis Cardinals to a victory over the New York Yankees to tie up the World Series at three games all. But in the seventh inning of the final game, the Cardinal ace was needed again. His teammates held a 3-2 lead, but the Yankees had the bases loaded and their star rookie, slugger Tony Lazzeri, waiting at the plate.

Alexander had not warmed up before entering the game in relief, but he threw only three pitches before signaling he was ready to face Lazzeri. His next few tosses would make baseball history.

The way the story came to be told and retold over the years, Alexander had to be awakened from the nap he was taking on a bench out in the bullpen. He had a reputation for partying after winning a big game, and the day before he had won one of the biggest of his career.

The real story was quite different. Alexander had not been celebrating after his sixth-game victory. His manager, Rogers Hornsby, had asked him to be ready to pitch a few innings the next day.

As he prepared to take over the job of pitching to the Yankees, Alexander was aware how dangerous a lineup the Yankees had. This was the team of Babe Ruth and Lou Gehrig. Every batter was a threat, and the rookie, Tony Lazzeri, was the newest star. Still, Alexander was the picture of nonchalance. He had been a star for a very long time. He had been the very best pitcher in baseball, and he wasn't quite finished yet. True, the veteran pitcher was nearing 40, and the smoke was gone from his fastball. But in its place was incredible control—and a curveball that broke like it had rolled off a table.

Alexander was over six feet tall, but he was not intimidating the way Ruth and Gehrig were. In fact, he looked somewhat comical, with his weathered face and a cap that seemed at least one size too small. There was nothing funny about the way he treated the threatening Lazzeri, though. Alexander simply ignored him. He wanted to make the rookie nervous. After all, though it was up to the aging pitcher to get him out, there was just as much pressure on the young hitter. With two out and the bases loaded, it was up to him to drive in the much-needed run. Even a walk would tie the score. But Grover Cleveland Alexander was not known for giving up many of bases on balls.

At last Alexander could not keep Lazzeri on

he writers in the press box waiting any longer. he reporters were there to record history, vhoever made it. And for a moment it looked as f Lazzeri would be the one. On the third pitch, vith the count at 1 and 1, he hit a long, long drive lown the left-field foul line. Yankee fans began houting, and the Cardinals held their breath. Vas it a grand-slam home run that would make azzeri an immortal hero? No. At the very last noment, just before the ball disappeared into he stands, it curved foul.

The runners returned to their bases. Lazzeri till had one strike left, and he had shown he ould hit Alexander. The wily veteran pitcher hen tempted Lazzeri with a sharp breaking urve on the outer corner of the plate, and the ookie swung awkwardly at it. Strike three! lexander had struck out Lazzeri.

Alexander held the Yankees in check for the ext two innings, and then he and the Cardinals vere world champions.

In his long career in the National League, lexander had thrown thousands of pitches. nd before he finally retired, he would throw housands more. But the one that he and base-all fans would never forget was the pitch that truck out Tony Lazzeri.

2
THE EARLY YEARS

'oung Grover :leveland Alexander 'ar right) with his ·arents, his sister, nd six of his ·rothers.

When 13 children are born into a family, thinking up names for all of them is not easy. And when 12 of them are boys, the task is even harder. William and Margaret Alexander were running short on names when their latest son was born at their farm near Elba, Nebraska, on February 26, 1887. So they decided to name him after the man who was then president of the United States—Grover Cleveland.

Years later, after her son had become the greatest pitcher in the National League, Alexander's mother talked about Grover's boyhood. "Dode didn't take to farming," she recalled, using Grover's family nickname. Mrs. Alexander went on to tell how her son would pick up rocks, instead of potatoes, when he worked in the fields. She had to keep mending his pants pockets because they were always filled to bursting with the stones he liked to throw at targets.

"I'd send him off to the farmyard to fetch some chickens or a turkey for the family dinner," she explained. "Dode would take out one of his stones and hit a chicken in the head. He got so good he could pick them off while they wer running around outside the hen house."

The way Alexander told it, he began develop ing his extraordinary pitching control as a bo by knocking clothespins off the neighbor's was lines with pebbles. Either way, Grover starte pitching young.

All the Alexander children went to a one room schoolhouse in Elba and then on to hig school in the bigger town of St. Paul. Youn Grover considered St. Paul, Nebraska, his home town, and folks there called him both Alex an Aleck. During his baseball career he would late pick up the nickname "Pete" as well. It was give him by other players when he fell from a buck board while on a hunting trip and landed fac down in the mud. They said he looked like fictional western character known as Alkali Pete

Nebraska had been a state for only 20 year at the time Alex was born, and it was still sparsely settled frontier. Until Grover Clevelan Alexander grew up and became a baseball hero William "Buffalo Bill" Cody, who brought hi

St. Paul, Nebraska, in 1900.

amous Wild West Shows to the East, was the est-known Nebraskan.

Alexander's family hoped he would study law nd follow in the footsteps of his famous name-ake, but he was not nearly as interested in ooks as he was in baseball. Still, he finished igh school in 1905 and, after a year of farming, 'as hired as a lineman by the local telephone ompany.

There were no paved roads across the flat lains and sand hills of Nebraska, but already elephone companies were putting up poles. oung Alexander was hired to string up the hone lines. Of course, he had to climb the sky-igh poles first. It was hard work, but Alex did ot mind. At least he had his weekends free. hat beat working on the family farm, a seven-ay-a-week job.

Around St. Paul, folks already knew that lex was the best pitcher in the county, and he 'as kept busy on weekends playing for local eams. Mostly, he pitched, but sometimes, to est his arm, he played in the outfield.

Despite his local success, Alexander was urprised to be offered a professional contract y Jap Martin, the manager of the Galesburg, linois, team, in the Class D Illinois-Missouri eague.

After he signed his contract, it did not take ng for the 22-year-old Nebraska farmboy to ecome a favorite in Galesburg. By mid-season e had won 15 games, almost half of his team's otal victories. But then, on July 27, 1909, the tory of Grover Cleveland Alexander almost nded. Alex was playing the outfield that day gainst a team from Pekin, Illinois. He led off the ighth inning with a single but was forced out at

William "Buffalo Bill" Cody, famed frontiersman and entertainer. His Wild West show, featuring Annie Oakley and Chief Sitting Bull, toured the United States and Europe.

second base when the next batter hit a groun ball. Trying to make a double play, the Peki second baseman, Chief Edwards, hit Alex ful force in the head with a ball hurled from only few feet away.

Alexander collapsed, flat on his back. Pekin player named "Spider" Diehl came run ning to his aid and saw that Alexander wa turning blue and choking on the blood pourin down his throat. Diehl lifted Alex by the feet an a glob of blood that was blocking his windpip came up. Almost immediately, Alex began t breathe again.

Alexander was alive—but just barely. Fo seven days he remained unconscious. Willian Alexander came from Nebraska to be at his son' hospital bedside. As soon as Alex could trave he and his father took a train back to Nebraska The 1909 season was over for the young pitche

For a while, it looked as if his whole baseba career was over. The blow to his head had dam aged the optic nerve, leaving Alex with doubl vision. When he tried to play catch with hi younger brother Ray, who later became a mino league pitcher in California, he saw two targets

That winter Galesburg, without making an mention of the injury, sold Alexander to Indian apolis. When he reported for spring training, h still couldn't see straight. Only by closing on eye could he focus on a single target—and eve that did not always do the trick. One day whil throwing batting practice, one of his pitches wa so wild that it broke the ribs of the Indianapoli manager, Charlie Carr, who promptly sent Alex ander to Syracuse in the New York State Leagu

The Indianapolis manager thought he wa making a smart move—until Alexander's ey ight suddenly returned to normal. As soon as e could see where the ball was going, he started vinning again. He racked up 29 victories at yracuse, 13 of them shutouts.

Even so, the major-league teams were doubtul and wary about Alexander's eyesight, and no ne bought his contract. Finally, the Philadelhia Phillies, a team that usually finished far own in the standings, picked Alex up in the ninor-league draft for only $500. At the time, it vas the least a big-league team could pay for a ninor-league prospect.

Alexander reported for spring training in 911 and was assigned to the second squad, nade up mostly of substitutes. They were led by veteran catcher, Pat Moran, who would one lay manage the Phillies. Moran was the first to ealize Grover Cleveland Alexander was going to e a superstar pitcher. He insisted that Phillies nanager Red Dooin give him a chance to pitch or the regular team.

Dooin finally gave in, but he picked out a ough assignment for the rookie. Philadelphia ad two major league teams then, the Phillies in he National League and the Athletics (now ocated in Oakland, California) in the American eague. Before each season began, the two hiladelphia teams would play a City Series. The thletics were winners of the 1910 World Series, nd pitching against them was certainly a tough est for the young Alexander. Pat Moran advised im, "You'll pitch five innings. They'll be murler, but you'll learn something." Instead, it was he Athletics who would learn something. Alexnder turned in five innings of no-hit ball, hutting out the world champions. Grover Clevend Alexander had made the team.

3

THE PHILADELPHIA STORY

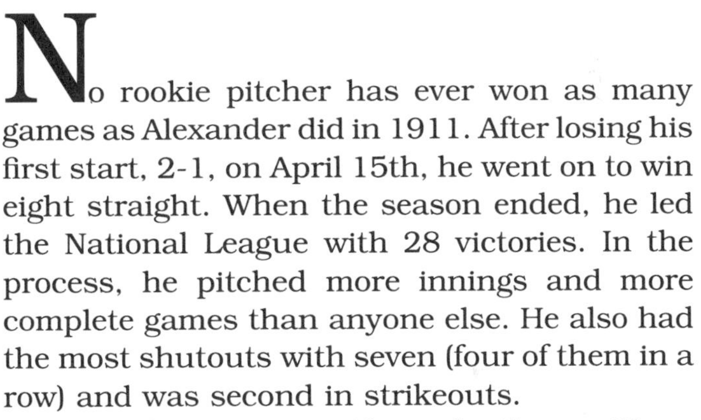

No rookie pitcher has ever won as many games as Alexander did in 1911. After losing his first start, 2-1, on April 15th, he went on to win eight straight. When the season ended, he led the National League with 28 victories. In the process, he pitched more innings and more complete games than anyone else. He also had the most shutouts with seven (four of them in a row) and was second in strikeouts.

From the very start, Alexander threw with an easy, almost sidearm motion. He bore down with an overhand fastball only when he needed to fan a batter. Although he became one of the top strikeout pitchers in the National League and led in that department in six different seasons, that first year Alexander was still developing his control. He walked 129 batters. By contrast, the future Hall of Famer Christy Mathewson, who was then nearing the end of his career with the

The Phillies pitching staff at the start of 1915. From left to right: McQuillan, Oeschger, Chalmers, Mayer, Rixey, Alexander, Demaree and second baseman Dugey. Between them, Alexander and Mayer pitched in 92 games in 1915.

New York Giants, walked only 38.

Alexander and Mathewson pitched agains each other three times. Although Alexander wor all three matchups, he was the first to admit tha his rival was past his prime when they met Their rivalry became a matter of Alexande trying to win more games in his career thar Mathewson had. When Mathewson retired ir 1916, he had 372 victories, a National Leagu record. The only pitcher with more victories was Cy Young, who won 511 games, pitching in both the National and American Leagues.

Most record books now show Mathewsor

and Alexander tied with 373 wins. A 1902 Mathewson victory was dropped from the official record because it came in a game when the distance from the pitcher's rubber to home plate was 6 inches less than the required 60 feet, 6 inches. Many years later, keepers of the official records restored the missing victory to Mathewson's record.

The next year, 1912, Alexander had a less successful season. Although he led the league in innings pitched and, for the first time, in strikeouts, Alex won "only" 19 games. Though that would have been a fine year's work for an

Philadephia's Baker Bowl, home of the Phillies until 1938. The eccentric ball park featured a hump in deep-center field caused by an underground railroad tunnel.

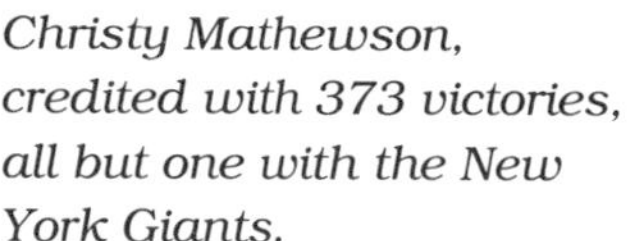

Christy Mathewson, credited with 373 victories, all but one with the New York Giants.

ordinary pitcher, Alexander had already shown that he was something special.

Alexander bounced back in 1913 with a 22-8 record, which included nine shutouts. These scoreless games became his trademark as he went on to shut out his opponents 90 times in his long career, still the National League record (Mathewson is second with 80). What makes his shutouts for the Phillies particularly impressive is the fact that he had to pitch in the smallest ballpark in the majors, Baker Bowl. The right-field fence was only 272 feet from home plate.

The whole rickety place would easily fit inside the modern Veterans Stadium, where today's Phillies play.

In 1914, Alexander again topped the league in victories, this time with 27 wins, while also leading in complete games and strikeouts. But that was nothing compared to his 1915 stats.

That year Pat Moran had been made manager of the Phillies and he was determined to lead the team to its first pennant. He relied heavily on Alexander, the league's most overpowering pitcher. Alexander won 31 games and was once again the league's strikeout king. Years later, Hall of Famer Frankie Frisch, in Larry Ritter's *Glory of Their Times*, recalled hitting against Alexander: "He had such an effortless motion, his fast ball sneaked. You'd get set, but it would be by you in the catcher's mitt. He mixed his pitches like nobody before or since, and if you tried to guess with him, you were a cinch to lose."

1915 was the first of three years in a row in which Alex would win 30 or more games. Although he never managed to pitch a no-hit game in his career, in 1915 he pitched four one-hitters. The 12 shutouts he pitched helped bring his earned run average down to a sensational 1.22, a major-league record that stood for 53 years until Bob Gibson recorded a 1.12 ERA in 1968. But, best of all, winning the pennant gave Alexander the chance to show what he could do against the top team in the American League, the Boston Red Sox.

4

ALEX MEETS THE BABE

The Boston Red Sox had a star pitcher of their own—a 20-year-old left-hander named Babe Ruth. Although he is now remembered for his home-run hitting, in his early years Ruth was the best southpaw hurler in baseball. As a rookie in 1915, he won 18 games for a team that had many fine older pitchers.

Alexander got off to a great start in the series opener, scattering eight singles and not giving up a run until the eighth inning. Then, for the first time, he met the Babe. Ruth was sent up to pinch-hit in the ninth inning with a man on first and two out. As Alexander later recalled: "I had heard he could hit the ball a long distance, so I didn't take any chances with him. He grounded out to the first baseman and that was his last appearance in that series." Though Alexander and the Phillies won that game 3-1, the Red Sox swept the next four, all by one-run margins. The Red Sox were world champions.

Alexander (right) and Ernie Shore of the Red Sox, the two starting pitchers in game 1 of the 1915 World Series.

The 1916 season was the best of Alexander's career. He won 33 games, two of them in a single day. On September 23rd, after Alexander had beaten Cincinnati, 7-3, manager Pat Moran came to him and said,"I'll have to ask you to pitch the second game, too. We've only a little more than an hour to catch our train back home. Get it over fast, will you?" Alex did as he was told, shutting out the Reds 4-0 in only 54 minutes.

In 1916, Alex led the league in ERA, games started and completed, and strikeouts. To top it all off, he had pitched an amazing 16 shutouts, which is still the all-time season record. According to Alexander he could have pitched even more: "I can remember at least three or four games of that season in which we had the other club beaten in the ninth and I had a shutout up to that point," he explained. "If I had pitched for shutouts, I know I could have had more of them."

But Alexander pitched to win, with as little

Alexander (back, left) with Phillies manager Moran and teammates Burns, Bender, Killefer (sitting on ground), and Luderus (kneeling), at spring training in St. Petersburg, Florida.

ffort as possible. If his own team scored runs arly, he would take it easy and save his arm. hat is one reason he was able to pitch so many ames.

In 1917 the Phillies again finished in second lace despite Alexander's 30 wins. Two of those ictories again came on one day—this time on eptember 3rd—in a doubleheader at Ebbets ield in Brooklyn. And again he led the league in ins, ERA, games started and completed, in-ings pitched, strikeouts and, as usual, shut-uts.

On the final day of the season, needing one nore victory to reach 30, he held a one-run lead n the ninth inning. But there were two out and he bases were loaded. Alexander's favorite atcher, Bill Killefer, came out to the mound. There's no place to put another runner," Killefer eminded Alex. The pitcher grinned and said, This'll make it 30 wins again, won't it Bill?" The atcher nodded his head. "Then we'd better get his batter out," Alex said, still smiling. And with hat, he reared back and fired three strikes to nd the game.

That strikeout was the last pitch Alexander vould ever make for the Phillies. Before the next eason began, he and Killefer would both be sold o the Chicago Cubs for a then record $65,000. The Phillies had been willing to sell Alexander's ontract because he was due to be drafted by the rmy.

5

ALEXANDER GOES TO WAR

Alexander's new team, the Cubs, had their spring training camp on Catalina Island, off the coast of Southern California; the team owner, William Wrigley, owned most of the island. It was the practice of the Cubs to attach several railroad cars to a westbound train from New York. Players and minor-league prospects would then board the train as it made stops along the way. Alexander, though he had yet to sign a contract with the Cubs, met up with the train in Kansas City. There he was interviewed by a young reporter from the *Kansas City Star*, Ernest Hemingway, who would later become one of the best-known novelists in the world. Hemingway wrote: "The mighty 'Alec' didn't sign a contract, but he checked his trunk through to California. Grover Cleveland may not sink his fins into any part of that $10,000 bonus he is demanding for attaching his monogram to a Chicago contract, but he isn't passing up any free trips to California."

Alex did sign his contract with the Chicago Cubs and won two games for them at the start of the 1918 season before beginning his military

.lexander arrives in ·ew York from ·rance aboard the ·ner Rochambeau. *"I ·hink I would have ·een a much better ·itcher today had it ·ot been for the War," ·e said in 1922. "I ·now I have never ·egained the pitching ·orm I had in 1917."*

service at Camp Funston in Kansas. There h joined the 89th Division, 342nd Field Artillery

Shortly thereafter, Alexander married Aime Marie Arrants, a woman he had met back hom in Nebraska the previous winter. They had gon out on a blind date arranged by friends in St Paul who had to explain to Aimee that Alex wa a famous baseball player. She had never heard of him.

Aimee and Alex were married on May 31st a Camp Funston. A few days later the 89th Division was sent to Camp Mills, near New York City to be shipped overseas. World War I was being fought in Europe, and the United States had already entered on the side of England and France to fight the Germans. Alexander was soon in France, part of the Allied assault that brought the Germans to surrender.

Before the fighting ended, Alexander spent seven weeks in the front lines, where he was constantly firing the big artillery cannons. As a result he became deaf in one ear. The damage he suffered has also been blamed for the headaches and epileptic seizures that afflicted him the rest of his life. But the terrible blow to the head he received in his first season in baseball, at Galesburg, might also have been the cause.

In any case, Alex came home from the war changed in many ways. He began drinking to ease his headaches and eventually became addicted to alcohol. Today we treat alcoholism as a illness. But then it was considered just a bad habit that the drinker could stop if he really wanted to.

Later, when Alexander's erratic behavior, such as disappearing for several days at a time, was blamed on his drinking, his wife, Aimee,

ould explain, "Almost always they were epilep-
ic seizures. He carried a bottle of ammonia and
ook sips when he felt a fit coming on." Aimee
ved her husband but hated his drinking, and
he couple had a stormy relationship. Although
hey would be divorced twice, she always sup-
orted him and remained his close friend.

The 1919 baseball season was ready to start
hen the troopship bringing Alex home docked
New York harbor. There to meet him was
Villiam K. Wrigley, the Chicago Cubs' multimil-
onaire owner. Wrigley used his influence to
ave Alexander discharged from the army al-
ost as soon as he came down the troopship's
angway. The two men rushed to Chicago by
rain so Alex could appear at the opening game
f the season. It had been a long time since he'd
hrown a ball, but he put on his Cubs uniform
nd threw the first pitch from the mound. Then
e left the park and began training so he could
in the team and take his regular turn.

Four weeks later Alexander made his first
tart, against the New York Giants at the Polo
rounds. For five innings Alexander held the
iants scoreless. Then he tired and was taken
ut for a pinch hitter after giving up three runs
the sixth inning. The final score was 3-2, but
lex was back and his performance was sure to
nprove. Sure enough, at the end of the season,
lexander's record was a respectable 16-11, and
is ERA was the lowest in the league. The Cubs,
owever, wound up in third place.

The next year, 1920, was Alex's first full
eason after the war. Now he was his old self
gain, the league leader with 27 wins. He also led
ERA, games started and completed, innings
itched, and strikeouts. However, Alex's pitch-

ing feats were overshadowed by Babe Ruth. Tha year the Boston Red Sox sold Ruth to the Ne York Yankees, where he became a full-tim outfielder—and a super-slugger. The Babe hi an astounding 54 home runs, demolishing th old record of 29.

Until 1920, pitchers were allowed to scuff u the ball, put saliva on it (the spitball), or do jus about anything to make the ball difficult to hit Baseballs were harder to hit for distance, and n matter how darkly stained or scuffed they got the balls stayed in the game. But then th owners decided that the fans wanted more scor ing and home runs. And so, to help the hitters all trick pitches, particularly the spitball, wer outlawed. Moreover, a new, much livelier bal was introduced.

Alexander, who had never marked a ball an had relied on his speed and sharp, natura curves, was forced to become a craftier pitcher He added a screwball, so he could make the bal curve in either direction, and began dependin

Alexander, catcher and manager Bill Killefer, and Speed Martin enjoy spring training on Catalina Island, California.

on his control, which had improved a great deal over the years.

To show off his control, Alex would warm up with his catcher, Bill Killefer, who would use a tomato can instead of a mitt. Bill would hold the can and Alex would plunk the ball into it. The catcher rarely had to move the target.

Unfortunately, Alexander was not nearly as controlled off the field. Chicago, in the 1920s, was the wrong place for someone with a drinking problem. While Americans like Alex were away at war, the 18th Amendment, making the manufacture and sale of alcoholic beverages illegal, had been added to the Constitution. Known as "Prohibition," it was just about impossible to enforce, and actually triggered widespread disregard for the law. In Chicago, gangsters, such as the notorious Al Capone, became almost a law unto themselves, and bootleg alcohol wasn't at all hard to come by.

But even as he continued to drink, Alexander continued to press toward his goal of passing Christy Mathewson in the record books. Matty had won 372 games in his career, and so Alex was determined to win at least 373.

In 1921, Alex's long-time catcher, Bill Killefer, was made manager of the Cubs. Once he realized that somehow Alex would show up when it was his turn, he let the pitcher follow his own rules—even if that included heavy drinking. In 1923, Alex won 22 games for the fourth-place Cubs. The following year, he missed half the season with a broken wrist, and the Cubs dropped to fifth. And in 1925, Alexander was 15-11, and his team finished last.

Bill Killefer was fired as manager in 1926. His replacement, Joe McCarthy, had never

played major-league baseball and, despite hi success as a minor-league manager, he wa resented as an outsider by many of the Cubs McCarthy would finally lead the team to a pen nant in 1930; and later, with the New Yorl Yankees, he would manage eight more pennan winners and win the World Series seven times But as a rookie manager in 1926, taking over last-place club, he was faced with a big prob lem—Alexander's drinking.

The Cubs shortstop at the time, Jim Cooney later recalled: "Grover Cleveland Alexander wa a great guy for drinking when the game was on There was a rookie catcher, and Alexander woul have a pint of whiskey in the kid's locker an sneak in to take a drink once in a while. Mc Carthy didn't like him."

When Alexander failed to show up to pitcl a game in Philadelphia, McCarthy sent hin back to Chicago and convinced the Cubs t cut the veteran loose. It seemed like the end o

Alexander is honored by the Cubs in Wrigley Field in 1925. Next to Alexander (right) is Baseball Commissioner Kenesaw Mountain Landis (center) and (on crutches) shortstop Rabbit Maranville.

Alexander's career.

One team, however, still wanted him. Bill Killefer was now a coach for the St. Louis Cardinals, and he urged Cards manager Rogers Hornsby to claim Alexander when the Cubs offered him to any National League team for the waiver price of $4,000. "He can still pitch," Killefer insisted.

Hornsby took Killefer's advice and got a real bargain. The Cards were in a hot pennant race when Alex joined them late in June and took his place as a starting pitcher. Now 39 years old, he was given an extra day's rest between starts, but he was often called upon to relieve other pitchers when they were in trouble. The nine games he won were a major factor in the St. Louis Cardinals' first National League pennant.

The New York Yankees were the American League champs in 1926, and that meant the two great stars, Babe Ruth and Grover Cleveland Alexander, would meet again in a World Series.

6 THE BIG PITCH–ALEX'S GREATEST TRIUMPH

Alexander had never seen Yankee Stadium until the Cardinals practiced there for the 1926 World Series. Before then, whenever Alex played in New York, it was always in the National-League parks, the historic Polo Grounds or Ebbets Field. The Yankees had played at the Polo Grounds until 1923 when they opened their own ballpark. The sports writers began calling Yankee Stadium "The House That Ruth Built" because the money people paid to see Babe Ruth was used to pay for it.

The two teams vying for the championship had been assembled very differently. The Yankees were owned by a millionaire, Colonel Jacob Ruppert. In 1920, he had bought Babe Ruth from the Boston Red Sox for $100,000. It was the most money ever paid for a player's contract. The Colonel's money had also bought future Hall of Famers Earle Combs, Herb Pennock, and Waite Hoyt. In addition, the Yankees had bought a high-priced rookie, Tony Lazzeri, who proved to be worth every penny they paid for him. In 1926 he batted in more runs than anyone else

Alexander (left) and pitcher Bob Shawkey of the Yankees, the starting pitchers in game 6 of the 1926 World Series.

except Babe Ruth. Lazzeri and Alex would be linked forever in baseball history by the time the 1926 World Series went into the record books.

The Cardinals, on the other hand, were owned by a St. Louis businessman, Sam Breadon, who would care enough about Alexander when hard times came to set up a private pension plan for the old pitcher. Breadon left the running of the Cardinals' business office to Branch Rickey, the man who later signed Jackie Robinson as the first black player in the major leagues. Rickey also invented the "farm system" of developing future big-league players on minor-league teams owned by the major-league team. Today, all big-league teams have their own farm systems, but in the 1920s it was a new idea. It had already provided the Cardinals with future Hall of Famers Chick Hafey and Jim Bottomley. Although not a product of Rickey's farm system, manager Rogers Hornsby had never played for any team other than the Cardinals. Grover Cleveland Alexander was, of course, an outstanding exception to the "home-grown talent" idea behind the Cardinal success.

The 1926 championship turned out to be one of the most exciting, suspenseful World Series ever played. Every game was won by a pitcher who today is in the baseball Hall of Fame. It is the only time this happened in a full seven-game series.

Cardinal manager Rogers Hornsby chose to start a tricky left-hander, Wee Willie Sherdell, in the opening game in New York. He had a hunch that Sherdell's slow curves would keep Yankee sluggers Ruth, Meusel, Gehrig, and Lazzeri off balance. Also, the right-field stands, where the left-handed power hitters, Ruth and Gehrig,

Catcher Bob O'Farrell clutches the ball after Lazzeri struck out with the bases loaded in game 7 of the 1926 World Series.

pulled the ball, were very close at Yankee Stadium. It was just 295 feet to home-run territory, with only a low railing separating the lower right-field stands from the playing field. Hornsby knew left-handed batters had more trouble with lefty pitching, so he sent Sherdell out to stop the Yankees.

The Yankees went with their ace pitcher, the thin-faced Herb Pennock. He had led the staff with 23 wins, and this day he was almost perfect. After giving up two hits in the first inning, he settled down and allowed only one hit for the rest of the game.

Sherdell gave up six hits, all of them singles, and kept the Yankees' big bats in check. But Ruth and Gehrig got base hits when they counted most, and the Yankees eked out a 2-1 victory.

Back in St. Louis the fans were unhappy

because the Cardinals had not used Grover Cleveland Alexander to pitch the opener. They cheered up considerably when the veteran took on the Yankees the next day.

A record World Series crowd of 63,000 filled Yankee Stadium for game 2. They came to see whether Alexander, the player who had been booted off the Cubs earlier that season, had reformed and recovered enough to pitch against the Yankees. And for a while it seemed as if he had not.

The 39-year-old Alexander got off to a shaky start, giving up three hits and two runs in the second inning. The Yankees got another hit

Alexander getting a drink of water between innings. Babe Ruth wrote about Alexander: "Just to see old Pete there on the mound, with that cocky little undersize cap pulled down over one ear, chewing away at his tobacco and pitching baseballs as easy as pitching hay is enough to take the heart out of a fellow."

heir fourth, in the third inning—but that was it. From that point on, Alex was invincible. He retired the next 21 men to face him, 10 of them with strikeouts. He stopped Babe Ruth in his tracks (0 for 4) although it took a sensational grab by player-manager Rogers Hornsby at second base to rob Ruth of a hit in the ninth inning. The final score was 6-2, St. Louis.

The next three games were in St. Louis, and the teams traveled there by train. Today, with teams in cities on both the Pacific and Atlantic coasts, ball clubs fly across the country in under five hours. But in the 1920s it took 36 hours—two nights and a day—by train just to reach St. Louis, Missouri, from New York.

The teams boarded the train at New York's Grand Central Station as soon as the Sunday game was over. The players had their meals in the train's dining car and spent the days playing cards, reading, and talking baseball. At night the porters converted the seats into beds so the players could sleep. The veterans got the more comfortable lower berths, while the younger players climbed to the upper ones. Superstar Babe Ruth had a whole compartment for himself.

In game 3, the Cardinals delighted their hometown fans by shutting out the mighty Yanks, 4-0. On the mound for St. Louis, Jesse Haines made his knuckleball dance. He held the Yankees to five singles, one of them by Ruth and two by Gehrig. Haines even beat the Yankees at their own game, contributing a big home run to the Cardinals victory.

With the Cardinals ahead in the Series, two games to one, the Yankees turned to their leader, Babe Ruth. As legend has it, the Babe found his inspiration in the person of 11-year-old Johnny Sylvester, gravely ill from a fall off a horse. Young Johnny told his father he'd like the Yankee slugger to send him an autographed baseball and to "see Babe Ruth wallop a homer before I die." The story goes that when Ruth heard about the boy's request he sent him an inscribed baseball. It said: "I'll hit a homer for you in Wednesday's game. Babe Ruth."

Ruth did even better than his word in game 4 walloping three home runs. He hit the first off the St. Louis starter, Flint Rhem, a 20-game winner. The Babe's third home run, off reliever Herman Bell, was lined into the upper bleachers in center field. It was the longest drive ever hit at Sportsman's Park. Altogether, Ruth and company blasted the Cardinal pitchers for a 10-5 win. Johnny Sylvester recovered from his illness, and the Series was tied at two games all.

Game 5 started out just like the opener—with Pennock and Sherdell back on the mound. And it ended up pretty much the same way, with the Yankees in front. It was a pitcher's duel that had the teams tied at 2-2 after nine innings. But then, in the top of the 10th, the Yankees pushed across another run on a long sacrifice fly by Tony Lazzeri to win it 3-2.

After the game, the teams headed back to New York. Again, they climbed aboard their Pullman sleeping cars, and this time there was a private compartment for Alexander. Old Pete, as he was now more widely known, would be pitching the first game back at Yankee Stadium, and the Cardinals wanted him to be well rested. For unless he won, it would be the last game. New York was ahead three games to two. One more Yankee victory and it would all be over.

The Cardinals jumped off to a three-run lead in the first inning of game 6. Though Alexander was not quite as sharp as he had been in the second game, he did not have to be: he held a 4-1 lead through six innings, and then St. Louis erupted with five runs in the seventh. Alex kept Ruth off base as the Cardinals once more tied up the World Series, three games apiece, with a 10-2 rout.

In light of what would take place the next day, it is well to consider what happened after Alexander's second victory. Manager Rogers Hornsby knew his veteran was ready for a well-earned victory celebration. Alex had already done more than his share, beating the mighty Yankees twice. So Hornsby told the veteran, "I just might need another inning or two from you tomorrow. Will you be ready?" And Alexander assured him he would.

Aimee Alexander who was in New York with her husband, was always upset when people said afterward that Old Pete had gone out celebrating after the game. "We had a couple of highballs in our hotel room, that's all, and went to bed early," she said. "Alex knew he might be needed in the last game."

The seventh and final game matched Waite Hoyt, easy winner of game 4, against Jesse Haines, who had shut out the Yankees in the third game. The New Yorkers scored first when Babe Ruth hit a home run in the third inning. But the Cardinals bounced right back to take a 3-1 lead in the fourth. It looked as if Alexander would be spending the rest of the game in the bullpen. But then in the seventh inning, the wear of throwing knuckleballs caused the skin on Haines's hand to tear and bleed. The Yankees

1914 Cracker Jack card

Alexander is congratulated by his Cardinal teammates after striking out Lazzeri.

had the bases loaded with two out, and the dangerous Tony Lazzeri at the plate when Haines came out.

Hornsby looked toward the bullpen and called Alexander into the game. The sight of old Alex strolling in has been described many ways. Alex himself later explained, "I was in no hurry. That young rookie, Lazzeri, was the one who had to be nervous."

As Hornsby recalled it: "I trotted about halfway out to the outfield to meet Alex. 'The bases are full,' I told him. 'Lazzeri's up and there ain't no place to put him.'"

"Yeah," Alex drawled. "Well, guess I'll have to take care of him then."

"Alex threw only three warmup pitches," Hornsby said. "Then he was ready. The first pitch was wide for a ball. Lazzeri took the next one for a strike. Then Lazzeri laid into the third pitch and it was home run all the way. The Yankees were on top of the dugout steps to run and meet Lazzeri at home plate. But we got a break. The wind pushed the ball a little to the left, and it was foul by about ten inches. Then lexander took care of Lazzeri. He struck him ut with a curveball."

Many people remembered that as the game-nding strikeout. But Alexander still had to hold he Yankees in check for two more innings. Herb ennock, who had already won two games for ew York, was now pitching in relief. For a while was a standoff as he held the Cardinals coreless, and Alex mowed the Yankees down in rder. Then, with two out in the bottom of the inth, Babe Ruth stepped up to the plate. Alex orked him very carefully, knowing that the abe could tie the score with one big swing. The ount went up to 3 and 2, and then Alex broke curve over the corner of the plate. Ruth watched go by. "Ball four," umpire Hildebrand called, nd the Babe trotted to first base.

"What was wrong with it, anyway?" Alex ollered at the umpire.

"Missed by this much, Alex," the umpire aid, holding his hands a few inches apart.

"For that much," Alex said, "you might have iven an old guy like me a break."

Then, on Alexander's first pitch to the next atter, Bob Meusel, Babe Ruth tried to steal econd. He must have thought he could take the ardinal catcher, Bob O'Farrell, by surprise, ut O'Farrell was ready for him. The alert catcher unned the ball to Hornsby at second base, and uth was tagged out. The 1926 World Series was ver. Alex had won two games and saved the inal one for the Cards. Moreover, he had finally ad his showdown with Babe Ruth and had held he great Yankee slugger hitless.

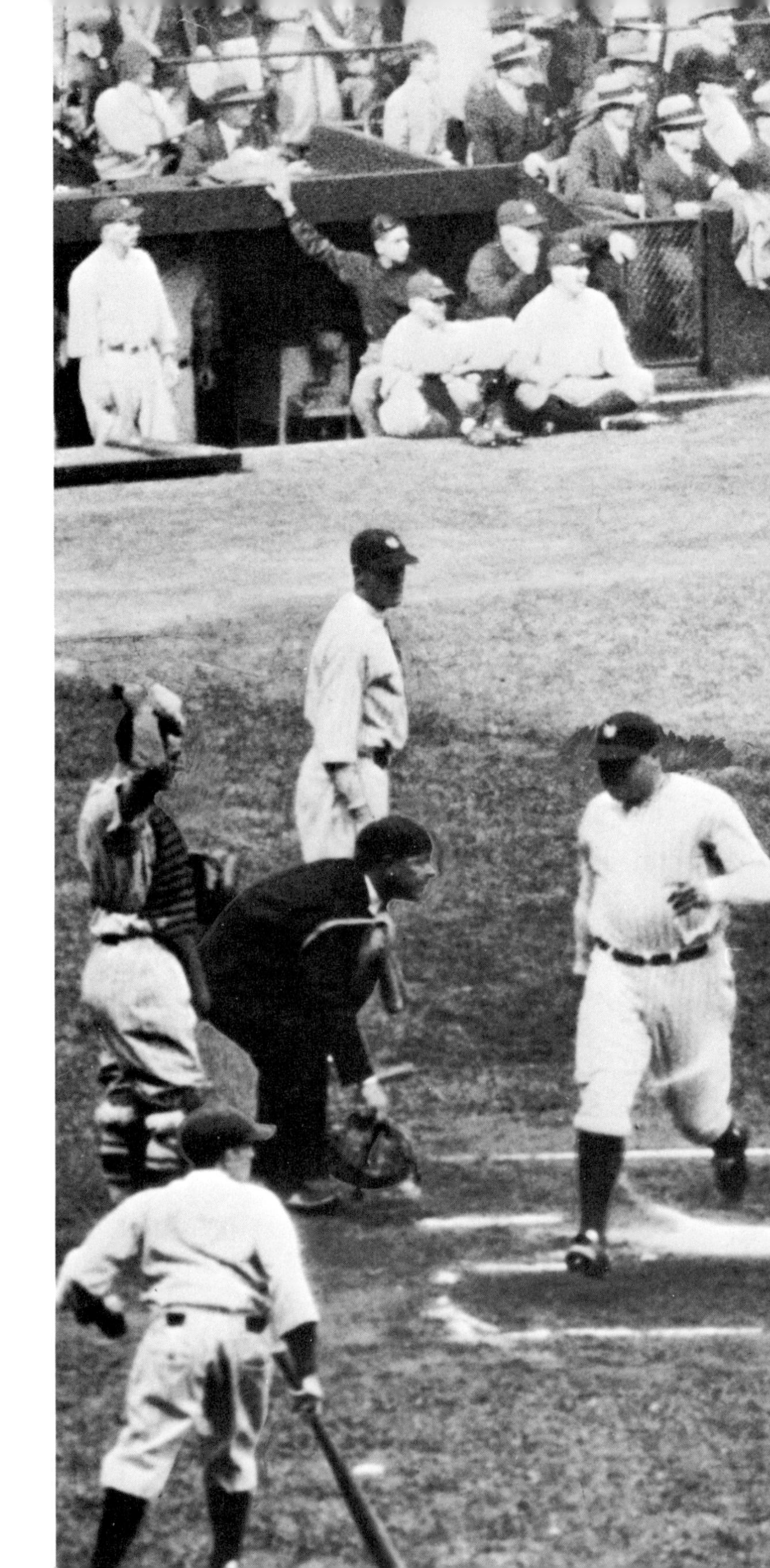

7

THE SUNSET YEARS

Thanks to his dramatic strikeout of Lazzeri, Alexander began receiving all kinds of offers. He turned down a trip to Hawaii to play exhibition games with a team of big leaguers. Alexander could have hit the vaudeville circuit (with its acrobats, jugglers, and other entertainers) to go on stage and talk about the Lazzeri strikeout. In later years he would do something like that, but right after the 1926 season all he wanted to do was go hunting with his friends.

In 1927 the Cardinals gave him a contract for $17,500. Only the manager, Hornsby, who also owned stock in the Cardinals, was offered more by the team. Babe Ruth, of course, received the highest salary in all baseball, and second to him was the American League's veteran star pitcher, Walter Johnson of Washington. But Alex made more than all other players—and he deserved it. Although the Cardinals failed to capture another pennant, Alex won 21 games for them, his first 20-game season since 1923, and was se-

Ruth scores after hitting his third home run, this one against Alexander, in game 4 of the 1928 Series. Ruth also hit three homers in one game in the 1926 Series, the first time any player accomplished this feat.

cond in ERA.

If Alexander broke training in 1927, it did not prevent him from pitching when it was his turn. He started 31 games and was often used in relief. He was now 40 years old, and time was running out for him in his race to break Christy Mathewson's record for most National League victories. At the end of 1927, Alexander had won a grand total of 348, but that was 25 short of his goal.

It became more difficult as he grew older. He still had superb control and could put the ball where the batter couldn't hit it squarely, but his legs were growing tired. Still, in 1928 he won another 16 games.

Meanwhile, St. Louis won another pennant and again took on the New York Yankees in the World Series. Once more, Alex pitched game 2 at Yankee Stadium. But this time he was wild, walking four men and giving up eight runs in less than three innings before being relieved. The Yankees easily won the game 9-3.

Babe Ruth had a fabulous World Series. In 1926 he had been walked 11 times. In 1928 the Cardinals elected to pitch to him, which turned out to be a mistake. The Babe batted .625, with 10 hits, three of them home runs. Once again, he got them all in one game, the fourth, in St. Louis. Alexander had been sent in to try to stem the tide in the seventh inning, but the Yankees could not be stopped. Ruth's final home run of the game was hit off Alexander, and game 4 turned out to be the final game as the Yankees swept the Series in four straight.

Alex had been pitching in the major leagues for 18 years, and the end of his career was in sight. Had he not lost almost a whole season to

Two future Hall of Famers, Cardinal manager Bill McKechnie (left) and Grover Cleveland Alexander. After the Cardinals lost the 1928 World Series, McKechnie was demoted to manager of the Rochester Red Wings.

the army in 1918 and a large part of 1924 to a broken wrist, he would long since have passed Mathewson's record of 372 wins. Instead, he still had to win those nine more games.

The 1929 season was a turbulent one for the veteran pitcher. Although at times he seemed like the Grover Cleveland Alexander of old, at other times he was clearly not himself. He would win a few, but then lose others. His drinking became an embarrassment to the team and to his wife Aimee. She divorced him, hoping that would straighten him out. And finally, in mid-season, Alexander agreed to enter a sanitarium for alcoholics. At that point he had won eight and lost eight and was one victory away from Mathewson's record.

After a month's rest, Alex returned to the team, clear-eyed and promising to stay sober. Bill McKechnie, the Cardinal manager in Alexander won 31 games and was once again th league's strikeout king. 1929 and a churc deacon, agreed to give him one more chance The team would be playing in Philadelphia, th very place where young Grover Cleveland Alex ander had begun his fabulous career in 1911.

On August 10, 1929, with the Cardinals an Phillies tied after nine innings, McKechnie sen Alexander into the game. "Hold them and we'l get you some runs," he promised. Alex used al his cunning and control to keep the Phillies i check for five scoreless innings, until his tean came through with the tie-breaker in the 14th He had finally won his 373rd National Leagu game. The National League's all-time record wa his.

Alex had many friends in Philadelphia, an they wanted to help him celebrate his histori achievement. "I won't take a drink, Bill," Alexan der promised manager McKechnie. And if h had thought there was a chance he would b needed the next day, maybe he wouldn't have But baseball was then forbidden to be played o Sunday in Philadelphia because of the so-calle "Blue Laws," which dated to America's coloni days and held Sunday to be a day of prayer Although the law was eventually repealed i 1934, in 1929 it meant that no professiona sports could be played on Sunday. As a conse quence, Alexander knew he would not be calle on at least until Monday.

"When he did show up on Monday morning he was a sad sight," McKechnie recalled year later. "Even so, I had him down to pitch Wednes day in New York, at the Polo Grounds against th Giants. I assigned one of our coaches, Gabb Street, as a bodyguard."

But as soon as the team arrived in New York, Alex disappeared. And when he showed up at the ballgame he was hammered out of the box. Reluctantly, McKechnie sent Alexander back to St. Louis. He tried to cover up for him by telling the owner, Sam Breadon, that Alex had a sore arm. Breadon was sure he knew the real reason, however. He paid Alexander for the final six weeks of his contract, and the veteran pitcher returned to his home in St. Paul, Nebraska.

HOUSE
OF
AVID

8
THE END

The Phillies decided to give Alexander a chance in 1930, after taking him in a trade for a couple of run-of-the-mill players, but the former 30-game winner had nothing left. After losing three games in relief, including a final one to his old teammates in St. Louis, Alexander was released. He then went to Dallas, in the Texas League, where he managed to pitch one last win in organized baseball before he was let go for failing to stay in condition.

Hard times were coming not only for Grover Cleveland Alexander but for the United States. The prosperity of the 1920s was followed by the Great Depression of the 1930s. Men all over the country lost their jobs and could not find new ones. A washed-up pitcher with a drinking problem had little to look forward to.

Alexander joined a touring team of semi-pros who wore beards and pretended to belong to a religious group called the House of David. Alex was not asked to grow a beard, just pitch an inning or two and coach. It was a living, of sorts.

Alexander with House of David player Dave Harrison.

Aimee came back, remarrying Alex in 1931,

and for five years she traveled with him and the team. But then, still in love but unable to cope with her husband's continual carousing, she gave up again.

Alexander began drifting from town to town, living on a small pension from the Cardinals, paid by Sam Breadon. Time after time Alex would pawn his World Series ring when he ran out of money, and then Breadon or Branch Rickey would redeem it. The ring had been presented to him and the other members of the 1926 world champions, in a ceremony at Sportsman's Park, St. Louis, during the 1927 season. Charles Lindbergh, known as "Lucky Lindy," who had become a great American hero by flying across the Atlantic Ocean alone in his plane, "The Spirit of St. Louis," had given out the rings.

In 1937, Alex had a brief moment of glory. It had been decided to build a baseball museum and Hall of Fame at Cooperstown, New York, and sportswriters began electing the members. Grover Cleveland Alexander was the sixth to be chosen. Only Ty Cobb, Babe Ruth, Honus Wagner, Walter Johnson, and Christy Mathewson were named before him.

In 1939, Alex got a steady job: he was put on exhibit at the kind of sideshow usually seen on a circus midway. This one, The Hubert Brothers Flea Circus, was in New York City, just off Times Square on tawdry 42nd Street. The owners charged a dime to people who wanted to see the main attraction, performing fleas, along with such freaks as the Fat Lady, the Tattooed Man, sword swallowers, and fire eaters. It bothered Alex to be part of such a set-up, but he needed the money.

On June 12, 1939, Alex arrived in Cooperstown, New York, to be inducted into baseball's

Still gripping a baseball, 53-year-old Grover Alexander watches the technique of sword swallower Nerelda Caswell.

Hall of Fame. Alex saw many familiar faces there, including Babe Ruth, still big and full of fun.

Following his induction into the Hall of Fame, Alex was once again a celebrity. There were times when he could earn a speaker's fee, but he could never get the job he really wanted. He always hoped to be hired as a coach by some team. Every so often the newspapers would report that he was in the hospital after a fall. They would hint it had been caused by his drinking, and sometimes it had. But epilepsy also plagued him.

In 1950, the Philadelphia Phillies won their first pennant since Grover Cleveland Alexander had pitched for them in 1915. He was invited to attend the World Series games when they played the New York Yankees. There were more interviews and newspaper stories, until he finally told

The hundredth birthday celebration of baseball in 1939 in Cooperstown, New York, attracted a lineup of stars. Left to right, front are: Eddie Collins, Babe Ruth, Connie Mack, and Cy Young. Left to right, rear are: Honus Wagner, Alexander, Tris Speaker, Napoleon Lajoie, George Sisler, and Walter Johnson.

the reporters, "I've gotten very tired of striking out Lazzeri."

Cancer now was added to the long list of problems Alex had to fight. He went back again to St. Paul, Nebraska, where he rented a room and spent his days writing letters to his beloved Aimee, who was then living in Omaha. On November 4, 1950, he mailed what would be his last letter to her. Then he went back to his room, and the next morning he was found dead.

The coroner wrote "heart attack" as the cause of death, but Alex had so many ailments it could have been almost anything. Aimee Alexander believed it was a final epileptic seizure and that, in falling, Alex had struck his head and died because

On the set of The Winning Team *are Rogers Hornsby (left), Aimee Alexander, and the movie's star, Ronald Reagan.*

ıo one knew he needed help.

Soon after Alexander was buried, with military ıonors, in St. Paul, Nebraska, the Warner Broth-ɛrs movie studio made a film about his life. Like nany movies about famous people, it strayed rom the facts. But Aimee served as a consultant on the movie and was flattered that her part was layed by Doris Day, a beautiful and popular ıctress and singer.

Until her own death, at age 87, in 1979, Aimee ıever missed a rerun of the movie, *The Winning Team*, on television. She always insisted that the oung actor who played her husband was not ıearly as handsome as Alex had been. She was glad when he gave up acting and went into politics. Ronald Reagan, who played Grover Cleve-land Alexander in the movie, became President of he United States in 1980. Alex, who had been ıamed for one president, ended up being played n a movie by another.

CHRONOLOGY

Feb. 26, 1887	Grover Cleveland Alexander is born in Elba, Nebraska
July 27, 1909	Suffers severe head injury during first minor-league season for Galesburg, Illinois-Missouri League
1910	Wins 29 games (13 shutouts) for Syracuse, New York State League
1911	Drafted by Philadelphia Phillies, wins 28 games and pitches 4 shutouts in a row
1915	Has first of 3 successive 30-game seasons. Phillies win pennant
Dec. 11, 1917	Sold by Philadelphia to Chicago Cubs
1918	Drafted into the U.S. Army
May 31, 1918	Marries Aimee Marie Arrants
1918	Serves military duty in France; is deafened by artillery guns
May 11, 1919	Returns to Cubs
June 22, 1926	Sold to St. Louis Cardinals
Oct.10, 1926	Strikes out Tony Lazzeri, N.Y. Yankees, with bases loaded, saving final game of World Series
1928	Helps pitch St. Louis to another pennant
Aug. 10, 1929	Wins 373rd game to break Christy Mathewson's N.L. record
Dec. 11, 1929	Traded back to Phillies by Cardinals
1930	Released by Phillies
1931-35	Tours with House of David, bearded semi-pro baseball team
1939	Joins Hubert Brothers Flea Circus
June 12, 1939	Inducted into baseball's Hall of Fame
Nov. 4, 1950	Dies, at 63, in St. Paul, Nebraska
1952	Movie biography, *The Winning Team*, is released, with Ronald Reagan playing Grover Cleveland Alexander.

GROVER CLEVELAND ALEXANDER

GREAT NATIONAL LEAGUE PITCHER
FOR TWO DECADES WITH PHILLIES,
CUBS AND CARDINALS STARTING
IN 1911. WON 1926 WORLD CHAMPIONSHIP
FOR CARDINALS BY STRIKING OUT
LAZZERI WITH BASES FULL IN
FINAL CRISIS AT YANKEE STADIUM.

MAJOR LEAGUE STATISTICS

PHILADELPHIA PHILLIES, CHICAGO CUBS, ST. LOUIS CARDINALS

YEAR	TEAM	W	L	PCT	ERA	G	GS	CG	IP	H	BB	SO	ShO
1911	Phil N	28	13	.683	2.57	48	37	31	367	285	129	227	7
1912		19	17	.528	2.81	46	34	26	310.1	289	105	195	3
1913		22	8	.733	2.79	47	35	23	306.1	288	75	159	9
1914		27	15	.643	2.38	46	39	32	355	327	76	214	6
1915		31	10	.756	1.22	49	42	36	376.1	253	64	241	12
1916		33	12	.733	1.55	48	45	38	388.2	323	50	167	16
1917		30	13	.698	1.86	45	44	35	387.2	336	58	201	8
1918	Chi N	2	1	.667	1.73	3	3	3	26	19	3	15	0
1919		16	11	.593	1.72	30	27	20	235	180	38	121	9
1920		27	14	.659	1.91	46	40	33	363.1	335	69	173	7
1921		15	13	.536	3.39	31	29	21	252	286	33	77	3
1922		16	13	.552	3.63	33	31	20	245.2	283	34	48	1
1923		22	12	.647	3.19	39	36	26	305	308	30	72	3
1924		12	5	.706	3.03	21	20	12	169.1	183	25	33	0
1925		15	11	.577	3.39	32	30	20	236	270	29	63	1
1926	2 teams	Chi N (3-3)		StL N (9-7)									
	total	12	10	.545	3.05	30	23	15	200.1	191	31	47	2
1927		21	10	.677	2.52	37	30	22	268	261	38	48	2
1928		16	9	.640	3.36	34	31	18	243.2	262	37	59	1
1929		9	8	.529	3.89	22	19	8	132	149	23	33	0
1930	Phil N	0	3	.000	9.14	9	3	0	21.2	40	6	6	0
Totals		373	208	.642	2.56	696	598	439	5189.1	4868	953	2199	90
World Series													
1915		1	1	.500	1.53	2	2	2	17.2	14	4	10	0
1926		2	0	1.000	0.89	3	2	2	20.1	12	4	17	0
1928		0	1	.000	19.80	2	1	0	5	10	4	2	0
Total		3	2	.600	3.35	7	5	4	43	36	12	29	0

FURTHER READING

Allen, Lee and Tom Meany. *Kings of the Diamond.* New York: G.P. Putnam, 1965.

Broeg, Bob. *Superstars of Baseball.* St. Louis, MO: The Sporting News, 1972.

Carmichael, John (ed.). *My Greatest Day in Baseball.* New York: A.S. Barnes, 1945.

Grayson, Harry. *They Played the Game.* New York: A.S. Barnes, 1944.

Grover Cleveland Alexander file, National Baseball Hall of Fame, Cooperstown, NY

Hornsby, Rogers and Bill Surface. *My War With Baseball.* New York: Coward, McCann, 1962.

Lieb, Fred. *Baseball As I Have Known it. New York*: Coward, McCann & Geoghagan, 1977.

Meany, Tom. *Baseball's Greatest Pitchers.* New York: A.S. Barnes, 1951.

Newcombe, Jack. *Fireballers.* New York: G.P. Putnam, 1964.

Reichler, Joseph (ed.). *The Baseball Encyclopedia,* 7th ed. New York: Macmillan, 1988.

Seymour, Harold. *Baseball: The Golden Age.* New York: Oxford University Press, 1971.

Seymour, Harold. *The Dictionary of American Biography,* Supplement IV. New York: Scribners, 1974.

Sher, Jack. *Twelve More Baseball Immortals.* New York: Bartholomew House, 1951.

Wray, John E. *Baseball's Greatest Lineup.* New York: A.S. Barnes, 1952.

INDEX

CTURE CREDITS

'/Wide World Photos: pp. 55, 57; Courtesy of the Family of Grover Cleveland Alexander: p.12; Courtesy of Levi Johnson: p.14; orary of Congress: P.15; Courtesy of James Charlton P.43; National Baseball Library, Cooperstown, NY: pp.2, 8, 20, 46, 60; UPI/ ttmann: pp. 18, 22, 24, 26, 28, 32, 34, 36, 39, 40, 44, 49, 52, 56, 58

JACK KAVANAGH, a free-lance writer of sports stories, began writing about sports as a high school correspondent for the *Brooklyn Eagle* in the 1930s. He has been a contributing editor to *Sports History* and his writing has appeared in various magazines, including *Sports Heritage*, *Vine Line* and *Diversions*. His work is included in *The Ball Players*, *Total Baseball* and other baseball anthologies. Mr. Kavanagh lives in North Kingston, Rhode Island.

JIM MURRAY, veteran sports columnist of the *Los Angeles Times*, is one of America's most acclaimed writers. He has been named "America's Best Sportswriter" by the National Association of Sportscasters and Sportswriters 14 times, was awarded the Red Smith Award, and was twice winner of the National Headliner Award. In addition, he was awarded the J. G. Taylor Spink Award in 1987 for "meritorious contributions to baseball writing." With this award came his 1988 induction into the National Baseball Hall of Fame in Cooperstown, New York.

EARL WEAVER is the winningest manager in Baltimore Orioles history by a wide margin. He compiled 1,480 victories in his 17 years at the helm. After managing eight different minor league teams, he was given the chance to lead the Orioles in 1968. Under his leadership the Orioles finished lower than second place in the American League East only four times in 17 years. One of only 12 managers in big league history to have managed in four or more World Series, Earl was named Manager of the Year in 1979. The popular Weaver had his number 5 retired in 1982, joining Brooks Robinson, Frank Robinson, and Jim Palmer, whose numbers were retired previously. Earl Weaver continues his association with the professional baseball scene by writing, broadcasting, and coaching.